Booze infused Cakes

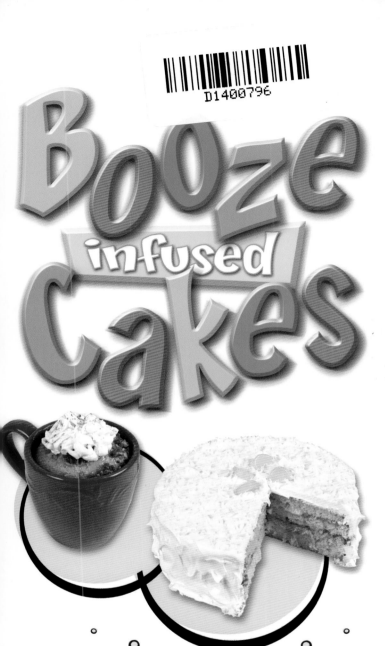

Intoxicatingly Delicious

I propose a toast!

Raise your ~~glass~~ plate and say "cheers" to the newest dessert idea – *booze infused cakes*. Already-delicious cakes are loaded with extra layers of flavor when liquors are added to batters, stirred into frostings, or injected into, brushed on or drizzled over baked cakes. From martinis and daiquiris to grasshoppers and tequila sunrises, your favorite cocktails have been bam *BOOZE* led and turned into intoxicatingly delicious cakes worth toasting!

 = *Ounces of liquor contained in entire recipe, not one serving.*

Printed in China

Published By:

CQ Products

507 Industrial Street
Waverly, IA 50677

ISBN-13: 978-1-56383-384-7
ISBN-10: 1-56383-384-0
Item #7061

Tipsy Tips to Remember

- Make guests aware of the alcoholic ingredients used in each dessert you serve.

- Although heat from baking or simmering reduces the amount of booze in a cake or sauce, it does not get rid of all of it. The flavor remains, as does some of the alcohol (5 to 85%), so these cakes are not intended for consumption by children and others who wish to avoid liquor.

Baking with Booze

- When adding booze to cake batter, you may replace some of the required liquid in the recipe, but for best results, don't replace all of it.

- Liquors may be used straight or stirred into a simple syrup made with equal parts sugar and water.

- To stir booze into fillings or frostings, add it in small amounts to maintain correct texture. Taste often! To boost flavor, supplement the booze with complementary flavored extracts as needed.

- Try poking holes into baked cake using a skewer, large fork or wooden spoon handle. Then gradually drizzle or brush booze over the top to add flavor and kick without over-soaking.

- A flavor injector works well to infuse booze directly into baked, cooled cake.

- For the biggest buzz, add alcohol to heated sauces or liquids AFTER they have cooled to room temperature.

Serve up some fun!

Harvey Wallbanger Cupcakes

Serves 18

Ingredients

1 (18.25 oz.) pkg. orange cake mix

1 (3.4 oz.) pkg. vanilla instant pudding mix

½ C. vegetable oil

½ C. plus 2½ T. orange juice, divided

⅓ C. plus 1½ T. *GALLIANO*, divided

4 eggs

2 T. *VODKA*

2 tsp. orange zest, divided

½ C. butter, softened

3 C. powdered sugar, sifted

hiccup...

Preheat oven to 350°. Line standard and/or mini muffin cups with paper liners; set aside. In a large mixing bowl, combine cake mix, pudding mix, oil, ½ cup orange juice, ⅓ cup *GALLIANO*, eggs, *VODKA* and 1 teaspoon orange zest. Blend on low speed until moistened. Increase speed to medium and beat for 2 minutes more. Spoon batter into prepared pans, filling cups about ¾ full. Bake standard cupcakes for 12 to 16 minutes or mini cupcakes for 7 to 10 minutes or until cupcakes test done with a toothpick. Cool cupcakes in pan for 5 minutes before removing to a wire rack to cool completely.

Meanwhile, in a large mixing bowl, combine butter and remaining 1 teaspoon orange zest. Blend on low speed. Add powdered sugar, remaining 2½ tablespoons orange juice and remaining 1½ tablespoons *GALLIANO*. Beat on low speed until well mixed. Increase speed to medium and beat until frosting is light and fluffy. Pipe or spread frosting evenly on cupcakes.

Drink your Harvey Wallbanger!

1 oz. vodka
3 oz. orange juice
1 oz. Galliano
Cherries and orange twist garnishes

In a mixing glass, stir together vodka and orange juice. Strain into a tall glass filled with ice. Top with Galliano and garnish with a cherry and orange twist.

Drink Recipe

forFun

Stack several cupcakes, cockeyed, in a tall drink glass. Garnish with additional orange zest and/or cherries and serve with a long fork.

Drunken Strawberry
Shortcake

Serves 8

6 C. sliced fresh strawberries

¾ C. plus 3 T. *AMARETTO*, divided

1 C. plus 2 T. sugar, divided

4 eggs, separated

¾ tsp. vanilla or almond extract

¾ C. flour

¼ tsp. cream of tartar

⅛ tsp. salt

1 C. heavy whipping cream

7½ oz. alcohol

Preheat oven to 325°. Line the bottom of an ungreased 9 x 9″ baking pan with parchment paper; set aside. In a large bowl, combine strawberries with ¾ cup *AMARETTO* and ⅓ cup sugar; let berries soak at least 30 minutes. In a large mixing bowl, beat egg yolks on high speed until very thick and lemon-colored. Reduce speed to medium and gradually beat in ⅔ cup sugar. Add 3 tablespoons water and vanilla; mix well. Beat in flour; set aside. In a small mixing bowl with clean beaters, beat egg whites until frothy. Add cream of tartar and salt. Beat until whites are stiff but not dry. Fold beaten egg whites into yolk mixture. Spread batter in prepared pan and bake for 22 to 25 minutes or until cake tests done with a toothpick. Cool in pan.

In a small chilled mixing bowl with chilled beaters, beat whipping cream and remaining 2 tablespoons sugar until soft peaks form. Fold in remaining 3 tablespoons *AMARETTO* (or less to taste). Cut cake into 16 squares. Place one square on each serving plate and spoon strawberries and juice evenly over cake, using half the berries. Top with another cake square and spoon remaining strawberries and juice over the cake. Add a dollop of whipped cream on top before serving.

Drink your Strawberry Shortcake!

1 oz. amaretto
1 oz. white crème de cacao
12 strawberries
2 scoops vanilla ice cream
Whipped cream

Drink Recipe

In a blender, combine amaretto, crème de cacao, strawberries and ice cream; blend until smooth. Pour into a hurricane glass and top with whipped cream.

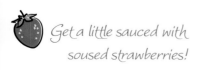

Get a little sauced with soused strawberries!

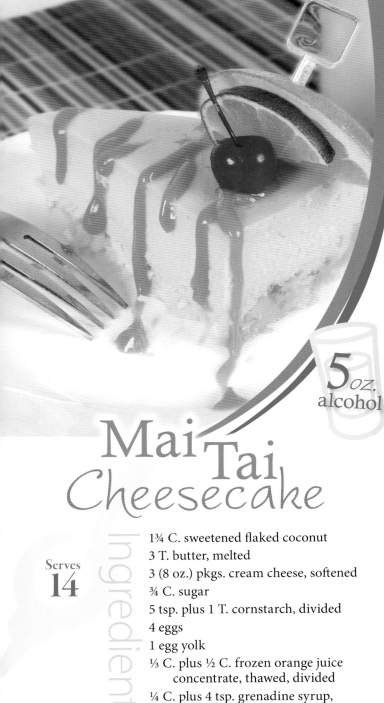

Mai Tai Cheesecake

Serves 14

Ingredients

1¾ C. sweetened flaked coconut

3 T. butter, melted

3 (8 oz.) pkgs. cream cheese, softened

¾ C. sugar

5 tsp. plus 1 T. cornstarch, divided

4 eggs

1 egg yolk

⅓ C. plus ½ C. frozen orange juice concentrate, thawed, divided

¼ C. plus 4 tsp. grenadine syrup, divided

¼ C. plus 1 T. *TRIPLE SEC*, divided

¼ C. plus 1 T. light *RUM*

2 tsp. clear vanilla extract

4 tsp. lime juice

*Loosely translated, Mai Tai
means "out of this world, the best".
In other words, "Mmmmm..."*

Preheat oven to 350°. Grease a 9″ springform pan with
nonstick cooking spray; set aside. In a small bowl, stir
together coconut and butter until well combined. Press
mixture into the bottom of prepared pan. Bake for
12 to 15 minutes or until golden brown. Let cool.

In a large mixing bowl, combine cream cheese, sugar
and 5 teaspoons cornstarch. Beat on medium speed
until smooth. Add eggs and egg yolk, one at a time,
beating well after each addition. Reduce speed to low
and beat in ⅓ cup orange juice concentrate, ¼ cup
grenadine, ¼ cup *TRIPLE SEC*, ¼ cup *RUM* and
vanilla until blended. Pour filling over crust. Bake for
15 minutes. Lower oven temperature to 200° and bake
for 70 to 80 minutes or until the center is almost set
but still jiggles slightly. Remove from oven and cool for
1 hour. Chill uncovered overnight.

In a small saucepan over medium heat, stir together
lime juice and remaining ½ cup orange juice
concentrate, 4 teaspoons grenadine and 1 tablespoon
cornstarch. Cook and stir constantly until glaze
is thickened and bubbly. Cook 2 minutes more.
Remove from heat. Whisk in remaining 1 tablespoon
TRIPLE SEC and 1 tablespoon *RUM*.

Run a knife around the inside edge of the pan, wiping
knife frequently. Remove pan sides. Cut cheesecake
into wedges and drizzle with glaze.

♦toServe

*Spike orange and lime slices and maraschino
cherries in triple sec for 30 minutes. Drain
well on paper towels. Garnish cheesecake
wedges with the spiked fruit.*

Blue
Hawaiian
Cupcakes

Serves
24

Ingredients

1 (18.25 oz.) pkg. white cake mix
¾ C. pineapple juice
½ C. light *RUM*
3 egg whites
⅓ C. vegetable oil
½ C. cream of coconut
2 T. *BLUE CURAÇAO*
1 (7 oz.) can Reddi-wip topping
Maraschino cherries with stems

5 *oz.*
alcohol

Preheat oven to 350°. Line standard muffin cups with paper liners; set aside. In a large mixing bowl, combine cake mix, pineapple juice, *RUM*, egg whites and oil. Blend with a mixer on low speed until moistened. Increase speed to medium and beat for 2 minutes. Spoon batter into prepared muffin pans, filling cups about half full. Bake for 20 to 25 minutes or until cupcakes test done with a toothpick. Cool completely.

Drink your Blue Hawaiian!

1 C. crushed ice
1 oz. light rum
2 oz. pineapple juice
1 oz. blue curaçao
1 oz. cream of coconut
Pineapple wedge and cherry garnishes

In a blender, combine ice, rum, pineapple juice, blue curaçao and cream of coconut; blend until smooth. Serve in a hurricane glass with a straw and garnish with pineapple and cherry.

Poke the end of a wooden spoon into the top of each cupcake, making one to three holes about ¾ the way through cupcake. In a small spouted measuring cup, whisk together cream of coconut and *BLUE CURAÇAO*. Pour mixture into the holes in cupcakes until filled; let stand for at least 10 minutes.

Before serving, top cupcakes with a swirl of Reddi-wip and garnish with well-drained cherries.

for Added Cheers

Garnish cupcakes with blue coconut. In a resealable plastic bag, combine ½ cup coconut and a splash of blue curaçao. Seal bag, shake and knead until coconut is evenly tinted. Spread on paper towels to dry. Sprinkle over the whipped cream topping just before serving.

6 *oz.*
alcohol

Skewered
Kamikaze
Shooters

**Serves
14**

Ingredients

1 (9 oz.) pkg. white cake mix

1 egg white

5 T. *LIME VODKA*, plus more for
brushing over cupcakes, divided

½ tsp. lime zest

5 T. *TRIPLE SEC*, plus more for
brushing over cupcakes, divided

½ tsp. orange zest

Orange food coloring

2 C. powdered sugar, sifted, divided

2 tsp. butter, softened, divided

Green food coloring

30 to 32 candy cherry balls

30 to 32 candy lime wedges

Preheat oven to 350°. Spray mini muffin pans with nonstick cooking spray; set aside. In a small mixing bowl, combine cake mix, egg white and ¼ cup water. Beat on medium speed until well combined. Divide batter evenly between two bowls. To one bowl, add 2 tablespoons *LIME VODKA* and lime zest; stir well. To the other bowl, add 2 tablespoons *TRIPLE SEC*, orange zest and enough orange food coloring to attain desired color; stir until well combined. Spoon batter into prepared pans, filling cups about ⅔ full. Bake for 8 to 11 minutes or until cupcakes test done with a toothpick. Remove cupcakes from pan and set on a wire rack. While still warm, brush green cupcakes with additional *LIME VODKA* and brush orange cupcakes with additional *TRIPLE SEC*.

In a small bowl, whisk together 1 cup powdered sugar, 1 teaspoon butter, remaining 3 tablespoons *LIME VODKA* and desired amount of green food coloring. In a separate small bowl, whisk together remaining 1 cup powdered sugar, 1 teaspoon butter, 3 tablespoons *TRIPLE SEC* and desired amount of orange food coloring. Icings should be thin; stir in additional booze if needed. Dip lime cupcakes in lime icing. Dip orange cupcakes in orange icing. Set upright on a wire rack until icing is dry, about 30 minutes.

To assemble, skewer one cherry ball and one lime wedge on each of 14 to 16 long party picks/skewers. Add one orange cupcake and one lime cupcake, iced sides up, poking skewer through the center of each.

Drink your Kamikaze!

1½ oz. vodka
1 oz. lime juice
1 oz. triple sec
Lime wedge and cherry garnishes

Fill a mixing glass with ice. Add vodka, lime juice and triple sec. Shake well and strain into a chilled cocktail glass. Garnish with lime wedge and cherry.

Drink Recipe

Like the drink they're named for, these little Kamikaze Shooters pack a punch.

Chocolate Martini Swirls

Serves 5

Ingredients

1 (19 to 22 oz.) pkg. milk chocolate brownie mix

2 eggs

½ C. vegetable oil

4 T. white *CRÈME DE CACAO*, divided

2 (3 oz.) pkgs. white chocolate instant pudding mix

3 C. milk

½ C. *VANILLA VODKA*

2 T. *CHOCOLATE CREAM LIQUEUR*

Chocolate curls*

7 oz. alcohol

Preheat oven to 350°. Lightly grease the bottom of a 10½ x 15½″ jelly roll pan; set aside. In a medium bowl, combine brownie mix, eggs, oil, 2 tablespoons water and 2 tablespoons *CRÈME DE CACAO*. Stir 50 strokes or until well blended. Spread batter in prepared pan. Bake for 15 to 19 minutes or until brownies test done with a toothpick. Let brownies cool completely in pan.

Empty both packages of pudding mix into a medium bowl. Add milk and whisk well until smooth and thickened, about 2 minutes. In a separate bowl, stir together *VANILLA VODKA, CHOCOLATE LIQUEUR* and remaining 2 tablespoons *CRÈME DE CACAO*. Add vodka mixture to pudding and whisk until well blended; set aside.

Cut out brownie rounds using three round cookie cutters in graduated sizes. For 8-ounce martini glasses, cut out five 1¾″ rounds, five 2½″ rounds and five 3¾″ rounds. (Adjust brownie sizes for glass size.)

To assemble, put a spoonful of pudding mixture in the bottom of each martini glass. Set the smallest brownie round on pudding, pressing one edge down so brownie rests in glass at an angle. Spoon a layer of pudding on top of brownie. Set a medium brownie round on pudding at the same angle as first brownie. Add more pudding and top with the largest brownie round. Spread a level layer of pudding over the top. Sprinkle with chocolate curls. "Martinis" may be chilled before serving with spoons.

* *To make thick chocolate curls, rub a large milk chocolate candy bar against a grater to shave off curls of chocolate.*

Each dessert is rich enough to serve with two spoons. Share it with someone you love!

B-52 Ice Cream Bomber

Serves 12

Ingredients

2 C. finely crushed chocolate graham crackers (about 11 rectangles)

5 T. butter, melted

3 C. chocolate ice cream

2 T. *IRISH CREAM*

6 C. vanilla ice cream, divided

1 T. instant coffee granules

2½ T. frozen orange juice concentrate, thawed

1½ to 2 T. *TRIPLE SEC*

Chocolate curls or orange slices

Preheat oven to 425°. Lightly grease a 9″ springform pan with nonstick cooking spray; set aside. In a medium bowl, stir together cracker crumbs and butter until evenly mixed. Firmly press mixture over the bottom and about 1″ up the sides of prepared pan. Bake for 5 to 7 minutes or until firm. Cool at room temperature for 20 minutes, then place in freezer for 10 minutes.

Meanwhile, in a large bowl, soften chocolate ice cream. Stir in *IRISH CREAM* to blend. (Mixture should resemble a very thick milkshake.) Spread ice cream mixture over cooled crust. Cover and freeze for 1 hour or until firm on top. When chocolate ice cream is firm, soften 3 cups vanilla ice cream in a large bowl. In a small bowl, combine coffee granules with 1 teaspoon warm water; stir to dissolve. Stir coffee mixture into ice cream to blend well. Spread coffee ice cream over chocolate ice cream in pan. Cover and return to freezer for 1 hour or until firm on top. When coffee ice cream is firm, soften remaining 3 cups vanilla ice cream. Stir in orange juice concentrate and *TRIPLE SEC* until blended. Spread orange ice cream evenly over coffee ice cream layer. Cover with foil and freeze for at least 4 hours or until firm.

Just before serving, wrap a warm wet towel around the side of pan for a few seconds to loosen cake from pan. Unhinge and remove side of pan. Slice into wedges and garnish with chocolate curls or orange slices.

Drink your B-52!

½ oz. Kahlúa (or other coffee liqueur)

½ oz. Irish cream

½ oz. orange liqueur (such as Grand Marnier or triple sec)

Pour each ingredient into a shot glass over the back of a cold spoon in order listed (without disturbing previous layer) to create three distinct layers of flavor and color.

Drink Recipe

for**Added Buzziliciousness**

Soak orange slices in triple sec for 30 minutes. Drain well on paper towels before garnishing cake.

Cosmopolitan
Caketail

Serves
20

Ingredients

1 C. dried cranberries, chopped, plus
   more for garnish

5 T. *TRIPLE SEC*, divided

2 T. plus ¼ C. *VODKA*, divided

1 C. butter, softened, divided

2 C. sugar

2 eggs, room temperature

3 C. flour

½ tsp. salt

2½ tsp. baking powder

¾ C. buttermilk

1 C. frozen cranberry juice
   concentrate, thawed, divided

Juice and zest from 1 lime

4 C. powdered sugar

5½ oz. alcohol

Soak half the cranberries in 2 tablespoons *TRIPLE SEC* and the other half in 2 tablespoons *VODKA* for 1 hour. Then drain off half the liquid. (Be sure to taste-test the drained liquid several times before discarding it!)

Preheat oven to 350°. Spray a 9 x 13″ baking pan with nonstick cooking spray; set aside. In a large mixing bowl, beat together ½ cup butter and sugar until fluffy. Add eggs, one at a time, and beat until well combined. In a medium bowl, stir together flour, salt and baking powder. In a separate bowl, mix together buttermilk, ¾ cup cranberry juice concentrate, lime zest and soaked cranberries with remaining liquid. Add dry ingredients and wet ingredients alternately to butter mixture and beat on low speed until well mixed. Spread mixture evenly in prepared pan and bake for 35 to 45 minutes or until cake tests done with a toothpick. Cool cake for about 20 minutes in pan.

In a small bowl, stir together remaining ¼ cup cranberry juice concentrate and ¼ cup *VODKA*; brush over warm cake. Cool completely.

In a large mixing bowl, beat together remaining ½ cup butter, lime juice (about ¼ cup), remaining 3 tablespoons *TRIPLE SEC* and powdered sugar until light and fluffy. Cut cake and pipe frosting on each piece. Garnish with additional dried cranberries.

Drink your Cosmo!

1½ oz. vodka
1 oz. triple sec
1 oz. cranberry juice
2 tsp. lime juice
Orange slice

Fill a mixing glass with ice. Add vodka, triple sec, cranberry juice and lime juice. Shake well and strain into a chilled martini glass. Garnish with orange slice.

Drink Recipe

forFun

Set a piece of cake in a chilled martini glass and garnish with a lime wedge.

Grasshopper
Cupcakes

Serves
30

Ingredients

3 C. flour

1 tsp. baking powder

½ tsp. salt

¼ tsp. baking soda

4 (1 oz.) squares white baking chocolate

1 C. butter, softened

2 C. sugar

4 eggs

1 tsp. clear vanilla extract

¾ C. sour cream

5 T. green *CRÈME DE MENTHE*, divided

½ tsp. mint flavoring

Green and yellow food coloring, optional

continued on next page

5 T. white *CRÈME DE CACAO*, divided
1 (16 oz.) can whipped white frosting
Andes mints, wedges or shaved*

Preheat oven to 350°. Line standard muffin cups with paper liners; set aside. In a medium bowl, stir together flour, baking powder, salt and baking soda; set aside. Melt white chocolate in the microwave, stirring until smooth; set aside. In a large mixing bowl, cream butter on medium speed. Add sugar and beat until light and fluffy. Add eggs, one at a time, beating well after each addition. Reduce speed to low and mix in vanilla and melted chocolate. Add flour mixture and sour cream alternately to the creamed mixture, beating until just combined. Divide batter evenly between two bowls. Into one bowl, stir 3 tablespoons *CRÈME DE MENTHE*, mint flavoring and a little green food coloring, if desired. Into remaining bowl, stir 3 tablespoons *CRÈME DE CACAO*. Use one spoonful of green batter and one spoonful of white batter side by side to fill each cupcake liner ⅔ full. Bake for 16 to 19 minutes or until cupcakes test done with a toothpick. Cool completely.

Spoon frosting into a medium bowl. Add remaining 2 tablespoons *CRÈME DE MENTHE* and 2 tablespoons *CRÈME DE CACAO*, stirring until well blended. Stir in yellow food coloring until frosting matches the green color in cupcakes. Dip the top of each cupcake into frosting, swirling to cover. Garnish with mint wedges and/or shavings.

* To make mint wedges, cut each candy in half and then cut diagonally to make four wedges from each mint. To make shavings, slice the edge of a mint thinly with a vegetable peeler.

Mint and chocolate... yummy and creamy like the real thing.

Straight-Up Bourbon Balls

Serves 14

Ingredients

- 1 C. semi-sweet chocolate chips
- 1½ C. finely crushed chocolate wafer cookies
- ½ C. finely chopped pitted dried plums
- ½ C. powdered sugar
- ¼ C. *BOURBON*
- ¼ C. sweetened condensed milk
- ¼ C. sugar or colored decorating sugar, optional

2 oz. alcohol

savor...

Melt chocolate chips in the microwave, stirring until smooth. Add cookie crumbs, plums, powdered sugar, *BOURBON* and sweetened condensed milk. Stir until well combined. Cover and refrigerate for about 45 minutes.

Using 1 tablespoonful dough at a time, roll the mixture in your hands to create smooth, round balls. Store in an air-tight container at room temperature for 24 hours to allow flavors to combine.

Before serving, roll the balls in sugar to coat, if desired. Serve at room temperature. Refrigerate for up to a week or freeze for up to a month.

Drink your bourbon straight up!

Pour a measure of bourbon into a brandy snifter or other glass, relax, savor the aroma and sip away.

Drink Recipe

toServe

Layer several bourbon balls in brandy snifters to savor the aroma and enjoy them like fine liquor served straight-up.

23

Dreamy Creamsicle Loaf

3 oz. alcohol

Serves
10

Ingredients

1 (9 oz.) pkg. white cake mix
1 egg white
½ C. orange juice
1½ tsp. orange flavoring
Neon orange gel food coloring
4 C. vanilla ice cream
    (white like Breyers)
3 T. *VANILLA VODKA*, divided
3 T. *TRIPLE SEC*, divided
½ C. butter, softened
1½ tsp. vanilla extract
3¾ C. powdered sugar, sifted
Orange decorating sugar

Preheat oven to 350°. Generously grease and flour two 5 x 9" loaf pans; set aside. In a small mixing bowl, beat together cake mix, egg white and orange juice. Stir in orange flavoring and orange food coloring as desired. Divide batter evenly between prepared pans. Bake for 12 to 14 minutes or until cakes test done with a toothpick. Let cool in pans for 15 minutes and then flip cakes out onto a wire rack to cool completely.

Soften ice cream in a large bowl. Line bottom and long sides of a clean loaf pan with parchment paper, allowing 2" to hang over long sides. If necessary, trim off the crown on both cakes. Set one cake layer in prepared pan. In a small bowl, stir together 1 tablespoon *VANILLA VODKA* and 1½ teaspoons *TRIPLE SEC*. Brush half of the liquor mixture over the cake layer. Pour remaining 2 tablespoons *VANILLA VODKA* into softened ice cream and stir until smooth. Spread ice cream over cake in pan. Top with second cake layer and brush with remaining liquor mixture. Cover and freeze for 4 hours or overnight.

In a medium mixing bowl, beat together butter, vanilla, remaining 2½ tablespoons *TRIPLE SEC* and powdered sugar until smooth and light. Dip bottom of loaf pan into warm water for 5 to 10 seconds and pull up on parchment paper to remove cake from pan. Set loaf and paper on a large plate. Spread frosting on sides and top of cake, working quickly. Sprinkle with orange sugar. Return to freezer for at least 1 hour. Remove parchment paper and set frozen loaf on a serving platter. Slice and serve cold.

Drink your Creamsicle!

½ to 1 oz. vanilla vodka
½ oz. triple sec
1 oz. orange juice
1 oz. half & half

Fill a mixing glass with ice. Add vanilla vodka, triple sec, orange juice and half & half. Shake well and strain into a martini glass.

Drink Recipe

Hot Buttered Rum *Cake*

Serves 6

Ingredients

1 C. butter, divided
1 (18 oz.) pkg. butter pecan cake mix
1 pt. butter pecan ice cream, softened
4 eggs
½ C. buttermilk
1 C. crushed pecans, divided
¼ C. brown sugar, divided
1 C. sugar
½ C. plus 1 T. *RUM*, divided
½ C. heavy whipping cream
2 T. powdered sugar
Dash of cinnamon, optional

$4^{1/2}$ *oz.* alcohol

Yummm... *Put a smile on your mug when you nip this hot drink look-alike.*

Preheat oven to 325°. Grease and flour six 10- to 12-ounce mugs*. Melt ½ cup butter in the microwave. In a large mixing bowl, combine melted butter, cake mix, ice cream, eggs and buttermilk; beat on low speed until well blended. Fill each mug about ⅓ full with batter. Sprinkle batter with approximately half of the pecans and half of the brown sugar. Pour additional batter on top of brown sugar, filling mugs about ⅔ full. Sprinkle remaining pecans and brown sugar over the top of each. Bake for 35 to 40 minutes or until cakes test done with a toothpick. Cool completely.

Drink your Hot Buttered Rum!

1 tsp. butter
1 tsp. brown sugar
Ground cinnamon, nutmeg, allspice to taste
Vanilla extract to taste
2 oz. dark rum
Hot water
Whipped cream and cinnamon, optional

Drink Recipe

In a mug, mix together butter, brown sugar, spices and vanilla. Pour in the rum and hot water and stir well. Top with whipped cream and a sprinkling of cinnamon before sipping.

In a small saucepan, melt remaining ½ cup butter, stirring constantly. Gradually add sugar and ¼ cup water; heat and stir constantly until well blended. Remove from heat and slowly stir in ½ cup *RUM*. Using a large fork, carefully poke holes deeply into cakes. Slowly pour about ¼ cup rum mixture over cake in each mug, allowing it to soak into the cake.

In a small chilled mixing bowl with chilled beaters, whip cream with remaining 1 tablespoon *RUM* and powdered sugar until soft peaks form. Top cakes with spiked whipped cream and sprinkle with cinnamon, if desired.

* Be sure mugs are ovenproof. Cake can also be made in a greased and floured 12-cup Bundt pan. Bake for 1 hour.

Hard Lemonade Layer Cake

5½ oz. alcohol

Serves 14

Ingredients

9 eggs, room temperature, divided
2½ C. flour
2 tsp. baking powder
½ tsp. baking soda
¼ tsp. salt
1 C. butter, softened, divided
4 C. sugar, divided
2 tsp. vanilla extract, divided
1¼ C. buttermilk
¼ C. cream of coconut
1 (11.2 oz.) bottle *HARD LEMONADE*
2 egg whites
½ tsp. cream of tartar
Juice from 1 lemon (2 T.)
1 T. finely grated lemon zest
1½ C. sweetened flaked coconut, divided
1 T. light corn syrup

Preheat oven to 350°. Grease and flour two 9″ round baking pans; line bottoms with parchment paper and set aside. Separate yolks and whites of 6 eggs. In a medium bowl, whisk together flour, baking powder, baking soda and salt; set aside. In a large mixing bowl, beat ¾ cup butter. Gradually beat in 1½ cups sugar, then egg yolks, one at a time. Add 1 teaspoon vanilla; set aside. In a small bowl, combine buttermilk, cream of coconut and ¼ cup *HARD LEMONADE*. Add flour and buttermilk mixtures alternately to the butter mixture, beating until blended; set aside. Using a clean mixing bowl and beaters, beat 6 egg whites until frothy. Add cream of tartar and beat until soft peaks form. Beat in ¼ cup sugar, until stiff glossy peaks form. Fold beaten egg whites into batter to blend. Divide batter between prepared pans. Bake for 35 to 40 minutes or until cakes test done with a toothpick. Let cool in pans for 10 minutes. Loosen edges and invert cakes onto a greased wire rack. Remove pans and turn cakes right side up; cool completely.

Combine lemon juice with enough *HARD LEMONADE* to equal ⅓ cup liquid and place in the top of a double boiler. Whisk in 3 eggs and ¾ cup sugar. Cook over simmering water (pan should not touch water) and stir constantly for 10 to 20 minutes or until mixture thickens and reaches 160°. Remove from heat and strain out lumps. Cut up remaining ¼ cup butter and whisk into mixture until melted. Stir in lemon zest. Cover lemon curd and let cool. Refrigerate until chilled and thick.

Cut each cake layer in half horizontally. Place one layer on a serving plate. Spread with ⅓ of the chilled curd and 2½ tablespoons coconut. Repeat with two more layers of cake, curd and coconut, ending with cake on top.

In the top of a clean double boiler, combine 2 egg whites, remaining 1½ cups sugar, ¼ cup *HARD LEMONADE* and corn syrup. Cook over simmering water and beat for 3 to 4 minutes on low speed. Increase speed and beat for 5 minutes or until frosting is shiny and smooth with soft peaks. Remove from heat and add remaining 1 teaspoon vanilla. Beat on high for 1 to 2 minutes or until thick. Immediately spread frosting over entire cake. Sprinkle with remaining 1 cup coconut. Cover and chill before serving.

Mini Mountain
Mudslides

Ingredients

¼ C. heavy whipping cream

1 T. light corn syrup

2 oz. dark chocolate, coarsely chopped

1 tsp. plus ¼ C. *MUDSLIDE LIQUEUR*, divided

2½ T. plus ½ C. sugar, divided

2½ tsp. vanilla extract, divided

8 (1 oz.) squares semi-sweet baking chocolate, coarsely chopped

¾ C. plus 3 T. flour, sifted

⅛ tsp. salt

½ C. butter, softened

3 egg yolks, room temperature

4 egg whites, room temperature

Powdered sugar, vanilla ice cream or whipped cream, optional

2 oz. alcohol

Line 6 cavities of an ice cube tray with plastic wrap, pressing down firmly; set aside. Place dark chocolate in a glass measuring cup. Heat cream and corn syrup to a boil in the microwave, stirring several times. Pour hot cream mixture over chocolate, let stand for 30 seconds and whisk until smooth. Stir in 1 teaspoon *MUDSLIDE LIQUEUR*, 1½ teaspoons sugar and ½ teaspoon vanilla. Pour chocolate mixture evenly into prepared tray. Cover and freeze for 3 to 4 hours or until solid.

Preheat oven to 425°. Generously butter six 6-ounce ramekins and place on a baking sheet. Combine semi-sweet baking chocolate, 1 tablespoon sugar and remaining ¼ cup *MUDSLIDE LIQUEUR* and microwave until chocolate is softened; stir until smooth. Cool. In a small bowl, stir together flour and salt; set aside. In a medium mixing bowl, beat butter on medium speed until creamy. Gradually add ½ cup sugar and remaining 2 teaspoons vanilla, beating until light and fluffy. Add egg yolks, one at a time, beating well after each addition. Add cooled chocolate mixture and beat until smooth.

In a medium mixing bowl, use clean beaters to beat egg whites until soft peaks form. Gradually beat in remaining 1 tablespoon sugar until stiff glossy peaks form. Gently fold ⅓ of the beaten egg whites and ⅓ of the flour mixture into chocolate batter. Repeat until all egg whites and flour are incorporated. Divide half the batter evenly between prepared ramekins. Place one frozen chocolate cube in the center of each ramekin; press down slightly. Spoon remaining batter over chocolate cubes to cover completely. Bake for 12 to 15 minutes or until edges test done with a toothpick. Do not overbake.

Invert warm cakes onto individual serving plates. Dust with powdered sugar or top with ice cream or whipped cream, if desired. Serve immediately.

toServe

Add color with sliced fresh strawberries or whole raspberries.

3½ oz. alcohol

Mint Julep
Cupcakes

Serves 16

Ingredients

1½ C. cake flour

1 C. sugar

½ tsp. salt

½ tsp. baking powder

¼ tsp. baking soda

6 T. buttermilk

2 eggs, lightly beaten

1 tsp. vanilla extract

4 tsp. green *CRÈME DE MENTHE*

1¼ tsp. mint extract, divided

½ C. butter, melted

4 C. powdered sugar, divided

⅓ C. butter

¼ C. plus 4 tsp. *BOURBON*, divided

1 (8 oz.) pkg. cream cheese, softened

Galloping gourmet! It's off to the races with these spunky cupcakes!

Preheat oven to 325°. Line standard muffin cups with foil liners; set aside. In a medium mixing bowl, stir together flour, sugar, salt, baking powder and baking soda. Make a well in the center. In a separate bowl, combine buttermilk, eggs, vanilla, CRÈME DE MENTHE and 1 teaspoon mint extract, stir well. Add buttermilk mixture and melted butter to flour mixture. Beat on low speed until combined. Increase speed to medium and beat for 3 minutes more. Spoon batter into prepared pans, filling cups about ⅔ full. Bake for 18 to 20 minutes or until cupcakes test done with a toothpick.

Meanwhile, in a small saucepan over medium heat, stir together ½ cup powdered sugar, ⅓ cup butter and 2 tablespoons water until butter melts and mixture is blended. Do not boil. Remove from heat and stir for 2 minutes. Whisk in ¼ cup BOURBON. When cupcakes are done, remove from oven and let cool slightly. With a fork, poke deep holes in the top of each cupcake. Drizzle some of the bourbon butter sauce over each cupcake, allowing it to fill holes. Repeat to use all sauce. Let cupcakes cool completely.

In a large mixing bowl, combine cream cheese, remaining 3½ cups powdered sugar, remaining 4 teaspoons BOURBON and remaining ¼ teaspoon mint extract. Beat on medium speed until smooth and creamy. Spread or pipe frosting on cupcakes. Cut plastic straws into 4″ lengths. Garnish cupcakes with mint leaves and insert straws to resemble small mint julep cocktails.

Drink your Mint Julep!

10 mint leaves (plus sprig)
1½ tsp. superfine sugar
Seltzer water
2½ oz. bourbon whiskey

Place leaves and sugar in a julep cup or old-fashioned glass. Muddle well until leaves break down. Add a splash of seltzer water. Fill with crushed ice and add bourbon; stir well. Garnish with mint sprig and serve frosty.

Drink Recipe

Tequila Sunrise
Bundt Cake

Serves 14

Ingredients

Maraschino cherries (about 16), well drained

3 T. plus ½ C. golden *TEQUILA*, divided

1 (18.25 oz.) pkg. yellow cake mix

3 eggs

⅓ C. vegetable oil

¾ C. plus 1 T. orange juice concentrate, thawed, divided

1 tsp. orange flavoring

Red gel food coloring

3 to 5 T. grenadine syrup

1 T. powdered sugar, sifted

5½ oz. alcohol

Gulp...

Preheat oven to 350°. Generously grease and flour a 9″ Bundt pan and set aside. If desired, soak cherries in 2 tablespoons TEQUILA. In a large mixing bowl, combine cake mix, eggs, oil, ¾ cup orange juice concentrate, orange flavoring and ½ cup TEQUILA. Blend on low speed until moistened. Increase speed to medium and beat for 2 minutes. Divide batter evenly between three bowls (about 1½ cups per bowl). Leave one bowl plain. Add red food coloring to second bowl to achieve a medium orange color. Add more red food coloring to third bowl to achieve a dark red-orange color. Drain cherries and guzzle any extra tequila (if you must). Place cherries in bottom of prepared pan, setting one cherry in each groove. Carefully spoon the plain batter into pan, covering cherries. Spread orange batter over plain batter to cover. Top with red-orange batter. Bake for 30 to 35 minutes or until cake tests done with a toothpick.

Remove cake from oven. Drizzle grenadine over the top of hot cake. Let cool in pan for 10 minutes. Carefully invert cake onto a wire rack and remove pan. Whisk together remaining 1 tablespoon orange juice concentrate, remaining 1 tablespoon TEQUILA and powdered sugar. Brush glaze over warm cake. Let cool completely. Slice cake into wedges to serve.

Drink your Tequila Sunrise!

Drink Recipe

4 oz. orange juice
2 oz. tequila
½ oz. grenadine syrup
Orange slice and
 maraschino cherry
 garnishes

In a tall glass with ice, combine orange juice and tequila; stir well. Tilt the glass and slowly pour grenadine down the side so it sinks to the bottom and slowly rises up through the drink. Garnish with an orange slice and cherry.

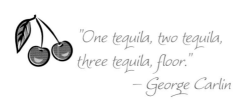

"One tequila, two tequila,
three tequila, floor."
– George Carlin

7 oz. alcohol

Chocolate Covered CherryShots

Serves 60

Ingredients

1 (3 oz.) pkg. cherry gelatin

1 (.25 oz.) env. unflavored gelatin

½ C. plus 3 T. white *CRÈME DE CACAO*, divided

2 T. *AMARETTO*

1 (18.25 oz.) pkg. devil's food cake mix

Vegetable oil and eggs as directed on cake mix package

⅓ C. maraschino cherry juice (or ⅓ C. water with 2 tsp. cherry flavoring)

⅓ C. *VANILLA VODKA*

1 C. heavy whipping cream

¼ C. sugar

Dissolve cherry gelatin in 1 cup boiling water. In a small bowl, sprinkle unflavored gelatin over ½ cup cold water; let stand 1 minute to soften. Add to hot gelatin mixture and stir to dissolve; cool to room temperature. Stir in ½ cup *CRÈME DE CACAO* and *AMARETTO*. Pour mixture into a 5 x 9″ loaf pan, cover and refrigerate 3 hours or overnight.

Preheat oven to 350°. Spray mini muffin pans with nonstick cooking spray; set aside. In a medium mixing bowl, beat together cake mix, eggs, oil, ⅔ cup water, cherry juice and *VANILLA VODKA* on low speed until blended. Increase speed and beat 2 minutes more. Spoon batter into prepared pans, filling cups about ⅔ full. Bake for 7 to 10 minutes or until cupcakes test done with a toothpick. Let cool in pans for 5 minutes before removing to cool completely. Poke cupcakes with a toothpick and brush tops with about 2 tablespoons *CRÈME DE CACAO*.

Use a sharp knife or tiny cookie cutter to cut gelatin into ¾″ cubes (approximately 60). Dip bottom of loaf pan in warm water for 10 seconds to loosen gelatin. Invert pan onto a platter and separate cubes; refrigerate until assembly. In a chilled mixing bowl with chilled beaters, beat cream with sugar until soft peaks form. Beat in remaining 1 tablespoon *CRÈME DE CACAO* until almost stiff. Place cupcakes into individual paper party cups. Pipe whipped cream on cupcakes and top with a gelatin cube. Serve promptly.

other**Flavors**

Quick & Dirty Margarita Shots
Prepare gelatin cubes as directed, using lime gelatin in place of cherry gelatin and substituting ⅓ cup *TEQUILA* and ¼ cup *TRIPLE SEC* for the crème de cacao and amaretto. Serve with yellow cupcakes and whipped cream spiked with 1 tablespoon *TEQUILA* or *TRIPLE SEC*.

Fuzzy Navel Shots
Prepare gelatin cubes as directed, using orange gelatin in place of cherry gelatin and substituting ¼ cup *PEACH SCHNAPPS* and ¼ cup *VODKA* for the crème de cacao and amaretto. Serve with yellow or orange cupcakes and whipped cream spiked with 1 tablespoon *PEACH SCHNAPPS*.

Pucker-Up Margaritas

Serves 4

Ingredients

1⅓ C. sugar, divided
¼ C. butter
¾ C. plus ⅓ C. lime juice, divided
Finely grated zest from 1 lime, divided
2 eggs, beaten
Green food coloring, optional
1 T. *TRIPLE SEC*
3 T. *TEQUILA*, divided
1½ tsp. unflavored gelatin
2½ T. orange juice
⅓ C. sour cream
⅔ C. heavy whipping cream
4 purchased round shortcakes
Lime slice, optional

2 oz. alcohol

It's 5 o'clock somewhere!

In the top of a double boiler over medium-high heat, stir together 1 cup sugar, butter, ¾ cup lime juice and 1 tablespoon lime zest until butter melts. In a small bowl, whisk eggs with 2 tablespoons hot lime mixture. Reduce heat until water simmers. Slowly whisk egg mixture into lime mixture. Cook until lime curd thickens and coats the back of a wooden spoon, 10 to 20 minutes; cool. Stir in food coloring, if desired, and set aside.

In a small glass bowl, stir together *TRIPLE SEC* and 1 tablespoon *TEQUILA*; sprinkle with gelatin and let stand for 1 minute. Microwave on high for 20 to 30 seconds or until gelatin dissolves. In a medium bowl, stir together ⅓ cup lime juice, orange juice and 1 teaspoon lime zest. Whisk in gelatin mixture. Place ice and water into a larger bowl, deep enough so the bowl with gelatin mixture rests in the water but does not submerge. Place bowl with gelatin mixture into ice water and whisk in sour cream until smooth; let stand 15 to 20 minutes, whisking occasionally, until mixture thickens. Meanwhile, in a small chilled mixing bowl with chilled beaters, beat whipping cream until soft peaks form. Fold whipped cream into thickened gelatin mixture. Refrigerate several hours or until mousse mounds when dropped from a spoon.

To assemble, mix several spoonfuls of sugar with remaining lime zest on a small plate. Coat the rims of four margarita glasses with lime juice. Dip rims in sugar mixture, coating well. Divide lime curd evenly between glasses. Top each serving with one cake, hollow side facing up. Brush cakes with remaining 2 tablespoons *TEQUILA*. Divide mousse mixture evenly between glasses, mounding it in the hollow of each cake. Garnish rims with a lime slice, if desired.

Raise your glass and shout "Olé!"

Toast to Champagne Cake

Serves 9

Ingredients

1 (18.25 oz.) pkg. white cake mix
2 egg whites
1 C. dry CHAMPAGNE, divided
⅔ C. maraschino cherry juice
1 C. heavy whipping cream
⅓ C. vegetable shortening (white)
4¼ C. powdered sugar, sifted
Pinch of salt
1 tsp. vanilla extract or cherry flavoring
Red gel food coloring
Coarsely crushed white or pink rock candy, optional

bubbly...

Preheat oven to 350°. Grease and flour two 8 x 8″ baking pans; set aside. In a large mixing bowl, combine cake mix, egg whites, ⅔ cup CHAMPAGNE and cherry juice; beat on medium speed for 4 minutes. Spread half of batter in each prepared pan. Bake for 20 to 25 minutes or until cakes test done with a toothpick. Remove from oven; let cool in pans for 10 minutes. Loosen edges of cakes. Invert and gently tap on pans to remove cakes; cool completely.

In a small chilled mixing bowl with chilled beaters, beat whipping cream on high speed until almost stiff; set aside. In a small mixing bowl, beat together shortening, remaining ⅓ cup CHAMPAGNE, powdered sugar, salt and vanilla until well mixed. Remove ¼ cup of frosting and tint it with red food coloring to reach desired shade of pink; refrigerate until serving time. Place one cake on a serving plate, top side up. Spread half of the white frosting evenly over top of cake. Set remaining cake on frosted layer, top side up. Fold whipped cream into remaining white frosting and frost sides and top of cake. Refrigerate until ready to serve. At serving time, cut cake and pipe reserved pink frosting on each piece. Sprinkle with crushed candy, if desired.

Champagne Chilled!

Chill Champagne to 45° by placing the bottle on ice for 30 minutes. Ease the cork out of the bottle and pour into long-stemmed flutes. Sip and enjoy the bubbles!

Drink Recipe

"Champagne is one of the elegant extras in life."
— *Charles Dickens*

Caramelicious
Appletini
Cupcakes

Serves 14

Ingredients

2 C. flour
½ C. sugar
1 tsp. baking soda
¼ tsp. salt
2 eggs, lightly beaten
½ C. vegetable oil
2 T. apple cider or juice
2 T. *VODKA*
¼ C. plus 3 tsp. *SOUR APPLE PUCKER SCHNAPPS*, divided
1 tsp. vanilla extract

continued on next page

4 oz. alcohol

1 C. Granny Smith applesauce
Green food coloring, optional
Green decorating sugar
2 T. butter
¼ C. dark brown sugar
2 T. milk
2 tsp. *BUTTERSCOTCH SCHNAPPS*, divided
2 C. powdered sugar, sifted
¼ C. half & half
15 caramels, unwrapped

Preheat oven to 350°. Spray mini muffin pans with nonstick cooking spray; set aside. In a large bowl, whisk together flour, sugar, baking soda and salt; set aside. In a separate bowl, whisk together eggs, oil, apple cider, *VODKA*, 2 tablespoons *APPLE PUCKER*, vanilla and applesauce until blended. Add egg mixture to dry ingredients and stir well. Stir in green food coloring as desired. Spoon batter into prepared pans, filling cups about ⅔ full. Bake for 7 to 8 minutes or until cupcakes test done with a toothpick. Let cool in pans for 5 minutes; remove to a wire rack to cool completely.

Pour 2 tablespoons *APPLE PUCKER* into a small bowl. Dip the top of each cupcake into the liquor and then dip into green sugar to coat; let dry on waxed paper. Meanwhile, in a small saucepan over low heat, melt butter. Add brown sugar and milk; cook and stir for 1 minute or until sugar melts. Remove from heat and cool slightly. In a medium bowl, combine butter mixture, 2 teaspoons *APPLE PUCKER* and 1 teaspoon *BUTTERSCOTCH SCHNAPPS*. Gradually add powdered sugar and beat until smooth. Beat in more *APPLE PUCKER* and *BUTTERSCOTCH SCHNAPPS* as needed, 1 teaspoon at a time, to reach a smooth piping consistency; set aside.

In a small saucepan over medium heat, combine half & half and caramels. Cook and stir until melted and smooth. Cool to room temperature.

toServe

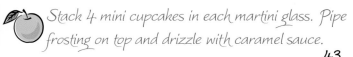
Stack 4 mini cupcakes in each martini glass. Pipe frosting on top and drizzle with caramel sauce.

Fuzzy Navel
Chiffon Cake

Serves 16

Ingredients

2¼ C. sifted cake flour

1½ C. sugar, divided

1 T. baking powder

¾ tsp. salt, divided

6 eggs, separated, room temperature

2 T. finely grated orange zest

¼ C. orange juice

½ C. plus 2 T. *PEACH SCHNAPPS*, divided

½ C. vegetable oil

2 egg whites

½ tsp. cream of tartar

½ C. heavy whipping cream

continued on next page

blitzed...

2 T. *TRIPLE SEC*
½ C. butter, softened
½ C. vegetable shortening (white)
4 C. powdered sugar
1 tsp. vanilla extract
Orange decorating sugar, optional
Spiked sliced peaches
    and/or oranges

Remove one oven rack and place remaining rack in the bottom third of oven. Preheat oven to 350°. In a large bowl, whisk together cake flour, ¾ cup sugar, baking powder and ½ teaspoon salt; set aside. In a separate bowl, whisk egg yolks, orange zest, orange juice, ½ cup *PEACH SCHNAPPS* and oil. Pour juice mixture over dry ingredients and whisk just until smooth; set aside. In a large bowl, beat 8 egg whites until frothy. Add cream of tartar and beat on high speed until soft peaks form. Gradually add remaining ¾ cup sugar, beating until stiff glossy peaks form. Fold ¼ of beaten egg whites into batter until just blended. Gently fold in remaining egg whites. Spread batter in an ungreased 10" angel food cake pan. Run a spatula through batter to eliminate any large air bubbles; smooth top. Bake for 40 minutes or until cake springs back when lightly touched. Remove pan from oven and immediately turn upside down on pan legs or a tall bottle. Let cool completely. Run a knife around inside of pan and center tube. Invert cake onto a large serving plate and remove pan.

In a large mixing bowl, cream butter and shortening on medium speed until light and fluffy, about 10 minutes. Add powdered sugar and beat until blended. Add remaining 2 tablespoons *PEACH SCHNAPPS*, *TRIPLE SEC*, vanilla, remaining ¼ teaspoon salt and cream; blend on low speed. Increase speed and beat until light and fluffy, about 5 minutes. Blend in a small amount of red and yellow food coloring to make light orange. Spread frosting over entire cake. Sprinkle with orange sugar, if desired. Garnish with sliced peaches or oranges. Chill before serving.

 Soak sliced peaches in PEACH SCHNAPPS and/or sliced oranges in TRIPLE SEC. Drain well before garnishing cake.

After-Dinner Drink
Drink
Cupcakes

Serves 24

Ingredients

1 (18.25 oz.) pkg. French vanilla cake mix

1 C. buttermilk

⅓ C. vegetable oil

4 eggs

1⅓ C. vegetable shortening (white)

1 C. sugar

2 tsp. vanilla extract

⅔ C. milk

½ tsp. salt

2 C. powdered sugar

Approximately 3 T. liquor mixture of each flavor (for every 6 cupcakes)

6 oz. alcohol

relax...

Peppermint Patty

Mix 1 tablespoon *CRÈME DE CACAO* with
2 tablespoons *PEPPERMINT SCHNAPPS*.
Unwrap 6 chocolate peppermint patties; set aside.

Golden Cadillac

Mix 1 tablespoon *GALLIANO* and 1½ tablespoons
white *CRÈME DE CACAO*.

Brandy Alexander

Mix 4 teaspoons *BRANDY* with 4 teaspoons dark
CRÈME DE CACAO.

Pink Squirrel

Mix 4 teaspoons *CRÈME DE ALMOND* and
4 teaspoons white *CRÈME DE CACAO*.

Preheat oven to 350°. Line standard muffin cups with
paper liners; set aside. In a large mixing bowl, combine
cake mix, buttermilk, oil and eggs. Blend on low speed
until moistened. Increase speed and beat for 2 minutes.
Spoon batter into prepared pans, filling cups about
⅔ full. Bake for 15 to 20 minutes or until cupcakes test
done with a toothpick. Let cool in pans for 10 minutes;
remove to cool completely. (To make Peppermint Patties,
set a chocolate patty on six warm cupcakes to soften;
spread over cupcakes and let cool.)

In a medium mixing bowl, beat together shortening,
sugar, vanilla, milk, salt and 2 teaspoons water for
7 to 8 minutes. Add powdered sugar and beat until
light and fluffy, about 5 minutes. Divide filling between
four bowls. Add 1 to 2 teaspoons of one liquor mixture
(listed above) to each bowl; mix and set aside. Fill
injector with one of the remaining liquor mixtures.
Poke the needle into a cupcake several times, avoiding
the center, and inject up to 5 ml. of liquor into six
cupcakes. Refill injector as needed. Repeat to make six
cupcakes of each flavor. Let stand for 20 to 30 minutes.

Using a pastry bag fitted with a long piping tip, pipe
filling into like-flavored cupcakes, finishing tops with a
swirl of filling. Make six cupcakes of each flavor.

toServe

*Poke a 4" straw into each cupcake, using
a different color for each flavor.*

6 *oz.* alcohol

Singapore Sling *Trifle*

Serves
8

Ingredients

1 (18.25 oz.) pkg. lemon cake mix (pudding type)

Vegetable oil and eggs as directed on cake mix package

¾ C. club soda

¼ C. *GIN*

1 (3 oz.) pkg. vanilla instant pudding mix

1½ C. milk

½ C. *CHERRY BRANDY*, plus more for drizzling

1 (21 oz.) can cherry pie filling (or more to taste)

Maraschino cherries

Preheat oven to 350°. Spray a 10½ x 15½" jelly roll pan with nonstick cooking spray. In a large mixing bowl, combine cake mix, oil, eggs, club soda and *GIN*. Beat on medium speed until well blended, about 2 minutes. Spread batter evenly in prepared pan. Bake for 10 to 14 minutes or until cake tests done with a toothpick. Let cool completely in pan.

Meanwhile, in a medium bowl, whisk together pudding mix, milk and *CHERRY BRANDY* for 2 minutes or until well combined and thickened. Cover and refrigerate until ready to assemble.

When cool, cut cake into about 100 (¾") cubes*. Place four or five cake cubes in each 10-ounce Collins glass. If desired, drizzle cake with ¼ teaspoon *CHERRY BRANDY*. Follow with approximately 2 tablespoons pie filling and 2 tablespoons pudding for each serving. Repeat layers of cake, *CHERRY BRANDY*, pie filling and pudding. Top with a few cake cubes and a maraschino cherry.

* Note: You will have extra cake.

Drink your Singapore Sling!

1½ oz. gin
1 oz. lemon juice
¼ oz. simple syrup
1½ tsp. powdered sugar
2 oz. club soda
½ oz. cherry brandy
Lemon slice and cherry garnishes

Pour gin, lemon juice, simple syrup and powdered sugar into a shaker with ice cubes. Shake well and strain into a highball glass with ice cubes.

Drink Recipe

Get a trifle tipsy from this dessert!

Tootsie *Cake* Roll

Serves 10

Ingredients

Unsweetened cocoa powder and powdered sugar for sprinkling

3 eggs, separated

½ C. plus 2 T. sugar, divided

5 (1 oz.) squares semi-sweet baking chocolate, divided

⅓ C. orange juice concentrate, thawed

1 tsp. orange flavoring or vanilla extract

¾ C. flour

1 tsp. baking powder

½ tsp. baking soda

¼ tsp. plus dash of salt

¼ tsp. cream of tartar

¼ C. butter, softened

continued on next page

5oz. alcohol

3 C. powdered sugar, divided
5 T. dark or white CRÈME DE CACAO, divided
5 T. TRIPLE SEC, divided
¾ C. whipped topping, thawed
2 T. orange juice
½ tsp. chocolate syrup, optional

Preheat oven to 350°. Line a 10½ x 15½" jelly roll pan with aluminum foil, extending foil 1" over pan edges. Grease and flour foil; set aside. Generously sprinkle cocoa powder and powdered sugar over a large tea towel; set aside. In a medium mixing bowl, beat egg yolks and ½ cup sugar until light, about 5 minutes. Melt 4 chocolate squares in the microwave, stirring until smooth; cool slightly. Stir chocolate into egg mixture. Add orange juice concentrate and orange flavoring, beating until smooth. In a small bowl, whisk together flour, baking powder, baking soda and ¼ teaspoon salt. Add flour mixture to chocolate mixture and beat until blended; set aside. In a large bowl using clean beaters, beat egg whites until frothy. Add cream of tartar and beat on high speed until soft peaks form. Gently fold chocolate mixture into egg whites until blended. Spread batter in prepared pan. Bake for 11 to 14 minutes or until cake tests done with a toothpick. Loosen sides of cake from foil. Immediately invert cake onto prepared towel. Peel off foil. Starting at a short end, roll up warm cake with towel inside, jelly roll fashion. Set on a wire rack to cool completely.

In a medium mixing bowl, beat butter until creamy. Melt remaining chocolate square; cool slightly, add to butter and beat well. Beat in dash of salt and ½ cup powdered sugar. Add 3 tablespoons CRÈME DE CACAO and 3 tablespoons TRIPLE SEC, beating on low speed until blended. Gradually beat in 1½ cups powdered sugar. Stir in whipped topping. Unroll cake and remove towel. Spread cake with filling, almost to edges. Re-roll cake without towel and freeze for at least 30 minutes.

Whisk together orange juice with remaining 2 tablespoons TRIPLE SEC, 2 tablespoons CRÈME DE CACAO, 1 cup powdered sugar and chocolate syrup, if desired. Slice cake and drizzle with orange sauce.

4^{1/2} oz. alcohol

Strawberry Daiquiri
Mini Cakes

Serves
16

Ingredients

1 (18.25 oz.) pkg. strawberry cake mix

3 eggs

1 C. frozen strawberry daiquiri mix
concentrate, thawed, divided

½ C. plus 1 T. *RUM*, divided

⅓ C. vegetable oil

¾ C. sugar, divided

2½ T. lime juice

2 egg whites, room temperature

¼ tsp. cream of tartar

1 T. light corn syrup

Dash of salt

1 tsp. vanilla extract

delish...

Preheat oven to 350°. Grease and flour five 4″ springform pans or 8 to 10 jumbo muffin cups; set aside. In a large mixing bowl, combine cake mix, eggs, ¾ cup daiquiri mix concentrate, ½ cup *RUM* and oil; beat on medium speed for 2 minutes. Divide batter evenly between prepared pans. Bake mini cakes for 24 to 25 minutes and jumbo cupcakes for 18 to 20 minutes or until cakes test done with a toothpick.

Meanwhile, in a small saucepan over medium heat, whisk together ¼ cup sugar, lime juice and remaining ¼ cup daiquiri mix concentrate. Cook, stirring until sugar dissolves. Remove from heat, let cool slightly and stir in 1 tablespoon *RUM*. Poke holes in warm cakes with a fork and brush the glaze over cake, letting it soak in. Cool completely on wire racks.

In the top of a double boiler, combine ¼ cup cold water, egg whites, cream of tartar, corn syrup, salt and remaining ½ cup sugar. Beat for 1 minute on medium speed. Place pan over boiling water (pan should not touch water) and beat on high speed for 7 minutes or until sugar dissolves and mixture reaches 160°. Remove pan from boiling water and add vanilla. Beat again until icing stands in stiff glossy peaks. Spread on cake and cut into wedges. Best when served the same day.

Variation

Use homemade or ready-to-spread strawberry frosting or vanilla frosting with 2 tablespoons daiquiri mix or *RUM* stirred in. If desired, sprinkle white sparkling sugar around the top edge of each cake.

Piña Colada
Upside-Down Skillet Cake

Serves 10

Ingredients

½ fresh pineapple, peeled, cored and cut into ¼″ pieces

1 C. *RUM*

¾ C. sugar

1 C. butter, softened, divided

5 eggs

2 tsp. vanilla extract

1½ C. flour

1 tsp. salt

¾ tsp. baking powder

1 T. brown sugar

continued on next page

10 *oz.* alcohol

¼ C. COCONUT RUM
¼ C. cream of coconut
2 T. whipped topping, thawed
Toasted coconut*, optional
Maraschino cherries, optional
Fresh pineapple wedges, optional

In a medium bowl, combine pineapple pieces and RUM. Cover and refrigerate overnight.

In a large bowl, beat together sugar and ¾ cup butter until creamy. Stir in eggs, one at a time. Mix in vanilla. In a separate bowl, stir together flour, salt and baking powder. Add flour mixture to butter mixture and beat until smooth; set aside.

Preheat oven to 350°. In a 10″ cast-iron skillet over medium heat, melt remaining ¼ cup butter. Add brown sugar, stirring to combine. Using a slotted spoon, transfer pineapple to skillet. (Sip the leftover pineapple-flavored rum while the cake bakes.) Cook pineapple for 10 to 15 minutes, stirring occasionally. Remove skillet from heat and let cool 5 to 10 minutes. With a spoon, remove any excess liquid. Pour batter evenly over pineapple in skillet and put skillet on center rack in oven. Bake for 30 to 45 minutes or until cake tests done with a toothpick. Remove from oven and let cool 5 minutes. Loosen edge of cake from skillet with a small knife. Place a large serving plate over the skillet and carefully flip the cake over onto the plate. Poke cake generously with a knife between pineapple pieces and slowly pour COCONUT RUM over the top so rum soaks into the cake. Let cake cool.

In a small bowl, stir together cream of coconut and whipped topping. Drizzle or spread over cake before slicing into wedges. Garnish with toasted coconut, cherries and pineapple wedges, if desired.

* To toast, place coconut on a baking sheet in a 350° oven for about 10 minutes or until evenly browned, stirring occasionally.

You're not blitzed — this cake really IS upside down.

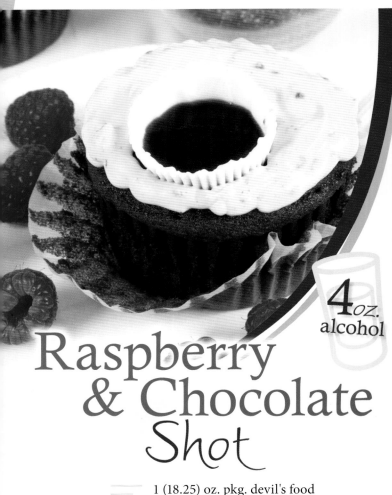

4 *oz.*
alcohol

Raspberry
& Chocolate
Shot

Serves
10

Ingredients

1 (18.25) oz. pkg. devil's food
  cake mix (pudding type)

Water, vegetable oil and eggs as
  directed on cake mix package

1 to 2 tsp. raspberry flavoring

1 (10 oz.) pkg. frozen
  red raspberries, thawed

1 tsp. unflavored gelatin

1 C. heavy whipping cream

¼ C. powdered sugar

½ tsp. vanilla extract

Red food coloring, optional

8 to 10 white chocolate
  shot glasses (p. 57)

½ C. *RASPBERRY SCHNAPPS*

Sweet...

Line 8 to 10 jumbo muffin cups with paper liners and set aside. In a large mixing bowl, combine cake mix, water, oil and eggs; mix as directed on package. Stir in raspberry flavoring. Spoon batter into prepared pans, filling cups ⅔ to ¾ full. Bake for 18 to 20 minutes or until cupcakes test done with a toothpick.

Drain raspberries, reserving 3 tablespoons juice. Press berries through a sieve to remove seeds and obtain about ¼ cup raspberry puree; discard seeds and set aside puree. Sprinkle gelatin over 1 tablespoon reserved raspberry juice; let stand 1 minute to soften. Boil remaining 2 tablespoons reserved juice and pour over gelatin; stir until gelatin is completely dissolved. In a chilled mixing bowl with chilled beaters, beat whipping cream, powdered sugar and vanilla until soft peaks form. Pour gelatin mixture into whipped cream mixture and beat until almost stiff. Carefully fold in raspberry puree and red food coloring, if desired. Refrigerate for 30 minutes.

With a small cookie cutter or knife, cut a round hole in the top and toward one side of each cupcake, as wide and nearly as deep as the chocolate shot glass. Frost tops of cupcakes with raspberry mixture. Insert a white chocolate shot glass in each hole and fill with 2 teaspoons RASPBERRY SCHNAPPS. To imbibe, hold the cupcake like a drink, bring it to your mouth, tip your head back and guzzle the SCHNAPPS. Eat the cupcake and shot glass as the chaser.

White Chocolate Shot Glasses

1 C. white chocolate baking chips (or other flavors/colors)
1 tsp. vegetable shortening (white)

In a microwave-safe bowl, combine baking chips and shortening. Microwave until melted and smooth, stirring every 30 seconds. Spoon 1 teaspoon of melted mixture into a mini muffin paper liner. With a small paintbrush, coat the inside of liner with a layer of chocolate, from bottom toward top edge. Repeat to make additional cups. Chill for 10 minutes or until set. Brush on a second layer and let dry. Before using, gently peel off paper liners. Set cups into holes in cupcakes and fill with booze.

4th of July

Shot glasses: Red shot glasses made from 30 red vanilla-flavored candy wafers

Cupcakes: White cupcakes. Poke holes and brush tops with vodka. Fill holes with grenadine.

Frosting: Ready-to-use fluffy white frosting and red/white/blue sprinkles

Shot of booze: blue curaçao

Santa Baby

Shot glasses: Red shot glasses made from 30 red vanilla-flavored candy wafers

Cupcakes: White cupcakes. Poke holes and fill with grenadine or green crème de menthe.

Frosting: Fluffy white or cream cheese frosting, stirring in mint flavoring to taste and a small amount of crème de menthe, if desired

Shot of booze: peppermint schnapps or green crème de menthe

Lemon Drop

Shot glasses: Yellow shot glasses made with 30 yellow vanilla-flavored candy wafers

Cupcakes: Lemon cupcakes. Inject each cupcake with about 5 ml. vodka.

Topping: Dip cupcake tops in lemon juice and then in coarse white sparkling sugar to coat generously.

Shot of booze: vodka

Polar Bear

Shot glasses: White chocolate shot glasses as directed

Cupcakes: Chocolate cupcakes with 1 to 2 teaspoons peppermint flavoring stirred into batter. If desired, inject cupcakes with peppermint schnapps and/or white crème de cacao.

Frosting: Fluffy white frosting

Shooter of booze: 1 teaspoon each peppermint schnapps and dark crème de cacao

Chocolate Heaven

Shot glasses: Chocolate shot glasses made with 30 chocolate candy wafers

Cupcakes: Chocolate cupcakes. In a small bowl, stir together 2 teaspoons each Irish cream, chocolate cream liqueur and Kahlúa; poke cupcakes and brush booze mixture over the top.

Frosting: Caramel frosting

Shooter of booze: ½ teaspoon each Irish cream, chocolate cream liqueur and Kahlúa

Tool Kit

Shot glasses: White chocolate shot glasses as directed

Cupcakes: White cupcakes. In a small bowl, stir together 1½ teaspoons each Irish cream, crème de cacao, amaretto and Kahlúa. Poke cupcakes and brush booze mixture over the top.

Frosting: Chocolate frosting

Shooter of booze: ½ teaspoon each Irish cream, crème de cacao, amaretto and Kahlúa

Index